Reflections of You

Jessica Cunningham

BookLeaf
Publishing

India | USA | UK

Presentation by *BookLeaf Publishing*

Web: www.bookleafpub.com

E-mail: info@bookleafpub.com

ISBN: 9789357444187

First edition 2022

DEDICATION

I have filled these pages with intent to share the Understanding, Love, and Grace I have been blessed with experiencing thus far, to be read by those of you who are feeling lost yet still hopeful to return to who You are at your Center.

This is for You.

And, for my children, who inspire me daily to keep learning and growing and teaching and shining.

To my dearest Jasmine and Preston:

I Love You.

I Saw You

I saw you at the corner store,
shining less than You.
I saw you there and wondered,
"What's the best thing I can do?

I could evade, I could drive off,
but I feel urge to stay,
for every time my gut's ignored,
there is a price to pay.

It may not mean trouble for me
in any coming days,"
but Something greater asked me
to slow down and heed Its ways.

I stopped by you, lowered the glass,
and greeted your response.
You asked me for four dollars,
for your Needs, not for your wants.

I told you Something moved me,
I'm so Joyful that I stayed,
and through the Guidance of our Core,
the greatest blessings made.

You smiled back, filling up my Heart,
and told me of your pain,
of all your recent obstacles
and all you Overcame.

I reached into my wallet,
praying for the right amount.
I counted ones, when I was done,
six was the final count.

I gave it to you on a prayer
that this would get you through.
I told you all you'll ever need
will find Its way to You.

Then You looked up and thanked Its Grace,
and so, I joined You there...
for what's been lost is always found
through Humbleness and Prayer.

I left knowing my time would come
to meet You once again,
through a stranger passing by
or time spent with a friend.

So, I looked up again and promised
I would stay the Course.
and signed,
your loyal Channel, Servant,

Guardian of the Force.

For those of us that carry Light
will often need help, too.
Just hold your Faith and head up High,
and It will come to you.

I Saw You (A Reflection)

Flying too close to the sun
will only burn your wings...

Just two days later, I succumbed
to how this Lesson stings.

I'd draped myself in gall and glory,
as I moved through Light.
I worked as sage, though merely novice,
fighting for what's Right.

I beckoned darkness to the stand,
although I was not ready...
came just enough to teach me that
I must Flow slow and steady.

And as the fear drew me in near,
I felt my Self depleting.
I lost my Grounding, for that fear
creates a Love that's fleeting.

I went down to the filling station

on an empty tank,
forgetting all that I'd just learned,
forgetting who to Thank.

I went to pay, and It declined,
and fear grew larger still.
I tried once more to no avail,
neglectful of Its Will.

I fell apart, clenched at my heart,
and tears obscured my face.
Then I looked over, and I saw You,
filling up with Grace.

I picked up all I could of me
and stumbled toward your side.
I asked You for four dollars,
as I wept through all my pride.

You nodded at me lovingly,
and pulled the nozzle out.
You brought it over to my tank
with zero shade of doubt.

I stopped it when my need was met,
although you'd stood back, waiting.
Six dollars was what you spent for
my rehabilitating.

I Thanked You, Thanked You, and again
and bowed my head to You.
I asked for blessings sent your way
for what You saw me through.

Then I surrendered to the Grace
of all You come to teach,
and I left, knowing that this Grace
is always within reach.

Sometimes We Fly, sometimes we fall,
but You are always there...
for what's been lost is always found
through Humbleness and Prayer.

Two Different Paths

Two different Paths
converged in Light
after their darkest season.
They came to Life
and danced along
without a need for reason.

The forest bloomed,
greens resurrected,
Light spread far and wide -
with such heat
and such passion
that comes when two stars collide.

They mirrored sunlight
off the trees
that thrived throughout the year.
Then other trees
grew denser leaves,
and Vision grew less clear.

And shade befell
this meeting point
through which these two Paths crossed -
Reflections of

last winter's death,
a repressed holocaust.

They knew they'd held
each other's ground
in many seasons past,
and so they promised
to each other
this was not their last.

They gathered sticks
and gathered stones
to fortify their surface,
forgetting that
rooting the soil
was of far greater Purpose.

The winds grew strength,
and Life evaded
as the ground was scarred.
But they kept building -
so they thought,
blinded to what they'd marred.

Every so often,
currents rose
and pulled the trees apart.
And at this time,
the Light shined brighter

on their crossroad heart.

Then they went digging,
leaving holes,
but finding buried treasures.
They spoke of Life
down by the River,
unknown sunlit pleasures.

As flowers bloomed,
they'd capsize them
to use to fill the holes.
Then rains would come
and break them down,
and they'd reset their goals.

Then Autumn came,
and only one Path
met Light at a time.
This one would grow
Its best to share
Its loving song and rhyme.

But when the lightened
Path would sing,
Nature came to obstruct.
Vines overgrew
each bend and slope,
as though to reconstruct.

Reflecting Light,
refracting dark
amongst each other's place,
Each Path when lit
now realized
that both were losing space.

Shared ground was worn,
the sun shone less,
and one Path grew uneasy.
It yearned for Flow
of water's edge,
a place well lit and breezy.

It reached out to
the other Path,
expressed Its need to move.
It asked the other
Path to spread
down to the River, too.

The other Path
inched its last stone,
then dimmed a little more.
And, through its vines,
it answered
with a fearful, quaking roar.

It knew just trees
and falling leaves
and Light that ever shifts.
It felt no comfort
traveling
to render unseen Gifts.

And so it stayed
immersed in trees,
rebirthing on repeat,
as its once mirror
flowed riverside,
free of Shadow's deceit.

The Human Race

All of Us
Springing off the walls we build
   and breaking them down as we're able
     and trading in time for discomfort
   and drifting through the clearances
And crashing into one another.

All of Us
Expressing different patterns of knowing
   and resolving our fears by Loving
     and balancing our chaos all alone
   and moving our grief into motive
and projecting our feelings awry.

All of Us
Reading and seeing and discerning
   and sharing and proudly rebuking
     and hearing and learning new ways
   and losing our minds to the clutter
and sorting it out in desperation.

All of Us
Affecting everything around us
   and carrying a Divine responsibility
     and fending off impulsiveness

and taking time to make choices
and understanding, or never at all.

All of Us
Creating the energy around us
    and absorbing the energy around us
       and vying to recreate it, whether
   to transmute it or repute it or use it
or abuse it, or Heal or harm with it.

All of Us
Building and destroying as we move
    and lifting or numbing as we speak
       and communing and dividing
   and growing and distracting
and searching for a Purpose.

All of Us
Living and working together
    and leaving scars as we drift
       and unlocking minds as we Flow
   and showing ourselves in the raw
and taking space to lose and gain.

All of Us climbing.
All of Us falling.
All of Us getting up to try again.

All of Us in this Together.

First World Problems

What is this way we treat our food
as though it's not required
to nourish, Heal,
and strengthen Us until our time's expired?

What is this nerve dysregulator
we sip to speed up?
A short-term focus, at the cost of muscle,
in a cup.

What is this rolled up thief of Breath
that we use to suppress,
but for a bullet to the lungs
and chemo for our stress?

What is this liquid that we drink
to drown our saddened minds?
A masochistic weapon
drawn to leave our Faith behind.

What is this costly capsule

we're assured will help us Heal
by taught and bought conveyors
who view sickness as a steal?

What is this lab-made substance that
We use to shrink our weakness,
but for facade of grandeur
leaving Head and Heart to bleakness?

What is this numbing needle that
we use to kill our pain,
but for a disconnection from our Instincts
as we drain?

What is this plant we burn up
so that we might learn to Fly?
Provided Sacred medicine
that only hoists so high.

What is this needless face paint
that we buy to cover Truth,
but for a way to mask what Is
or flee to shades of youth?

What is this garb we're wearing
to feel different - or the same,
but coverage made of Earth and toil
for status in a game?

What is this rock that we don
to contract us with a lover,
but for a taste for trend,
forged through enslavement of another?

What is this yearning
to use and abuse Autonomy?
A drive to have control
of something in you,
not in me.

What is this voice that's telling us
to hoard what we don't need,
but sneaky salesmen selling lies
and profiting from greed?

What is this paper construct that
we chase 'til bodies weaken,
but for exchange of goods
that we could share as Loving beacon?

What is this temperamental screen
that we use to distract,
but for a harmful glow
that hinders Thought from staying in tact?

What is this mode of information
seeking to divide Us?
The smoke and mirrors rerouting us

from seeking what's inside Us.

What is this written errant doctrine
that we use to war,
but for a Guide given as gift
to move us to learn more?

What is this pride that keeps us
acting out then caving in,
but for a faulty step stool
we climb to ascend our Kin?

What is this leach of Life
upheld by billions hunched to bear it,
but for a Calling to stand up,
and strip it of its merit?

What is this fear that steals our Joy
then guises theft as norm?
A desperate snake in winter
sucking from Us to keep warm.

What is this wound that moves us to
repress those we could Teach?
A stark reminder:
Heal Us first to lift those within reach.

What is this chaos that we seek
when we just need refilling,

but Insight that a simple change
will Rebirth all those willing?

What is this Present moment,
but a chance to start anew?
We came with everything We need.
It's all inside of You.

I Break for Bananas

Hello, my sweet and loyal friend...
A pleasure, meeting once again.
I chose you at the local store,
along with roughly twenty more.

I set your clan down on my table,
flipped you all so you'd be stable,
left you there, and let you age
until you'd reached the perfect stage.

I watched your green turn speckled yellow...
Now, a wholesome, freckled fellow...
So I plucked you, slow and steady,
knowing this is when you're ready.

But, before I eat you, listen close...
There's reason why I love you most.
You've always been right there for me,
and we've stayed close through history.

For when I couldn't sleep at night,
you'd comfort and relax me right.
And when I was too weak to stand,
your nutrients would take my hand.

Not only that, but every time
my muscles ached or gave a sign
that my Breath needed extra wind,
you were my greatest Medicine.

You are the fruit that I trust best
to keep me fueled and free from stress.
I cherish your potassium,
as oft it's helped me overcome.

Yes, you, sir, are my Grace right now.
I'll take your jacket, then I'll bow,
appreciating you for seeding
all the strength that I'm now needing.

I'm inspired to make you famous...
all your parts, except your anus.
That part's gross, but that's okay.
You're such a blessing, anyway.

Since you're organic, I can use
every bit, 'cept butt or bruise...
I'll chew the rest and save your peel
to make tea after my last meal.

Your peel, well, that's another story
of magnesium-rich glory,
soothing nerves and busy brain,
repairing cells, reducing pain...

A wise and lovely friend once said,
"Whenever leaving your homestead,
bring a banana just in case
you need a snack to feed your face."

So, every morn, I prep my fix...
I pack up one, or two, or six,
and thank the seed from which you grew
for replenishing me through all I do.

I wish for all the world to know
of all the Joyfulness you sow,
and everything your produce friends
can do for us to help us mend.

You're one of many offerings
the Mother gives to grow us wings.
The closer We eat, the higher We soar.
Remember this, next time, at the store.

If banana, broccoli, squash, or pear,
blues, reds, greens, yellows: say a Prayer,
'cause speaking Love to what We eat
makes for an extra Loving treat.

Two Different Paths
(The Surrender)

One Autumn,
there within the woods,
the shadowed Path stood still.
It felt that
same uneasiness
the Lighted Path instilled.

The seasons came,
the seasons went,
yet this one broke the mold.
The shadowed Path
missed sunlight
and grew tired of Shadow's cold.

The Path now at
the River's edge
beckoned to Its old friend.
"The water's calm,
the breeze is smooth,
come meet Me once again."

It looked down to

the Lighted Path,
and saw the flowers in bloom.
It wondered,
if it ventured there,
if there'd be any room.

The Lighted Path
sent smiles upwind
and warmed the tree-scaped view.
It then said to
Its fearful friend,
"Completely up to you...

The River flows
in one direction,
but there's so much space
and so much Love,
and open air
to Flow at your own pace.

I've saved you land
to course upon,
I've not forgotten You.
We dance and glow
and labor
in a way We never knew.

The Light here's
unpolluted space

where no one seems to tread,
except for
brilliant, wild Life
that are here to mend instead."

It felt the Grace
of making moves
and sent this Love uphill -
respecting choice
of others
to adhere to their own will.

Then winter came,
and winter left.
The sun came out once more.
The shade still dimmed
amongst the trees,
and vines choked out the floor.

The shadowed Path
felt overwrought
and also felt ashamed
for letting all those
seasons pass,
gifted land go unclaimed.

Humbled,
it then lightly dug
a step beyond the trees.

It felt the freshness
of the air
and comfort of the breeze.

It saw its first
butterfly perch
onto a budding rose.
It heard the water
giving Life
to everything that grows.

It thought winter
need not be such
a spectacle of death,
and felt it needed
more Light for its soil
and for its Breath.

The Lighted Path
just watched in glee
and placed some stepping stones
to guide Its brave
and curious friend
down toward their River home.

Then suddenly,
the skies turned gray.
The growing Path grew scared.
The Lighted Path

had warned before
that one should be prepared...

For sometimes rain
or storms would come,
but neither need to fear,
for even without treescape,
when the fog lifts,
They'll be Here.

The growing Path
still quaked
as thunder echoed through the air.
The step stones now
seemed farther
than it could spread, should it dare.

The Path down at
the River's edge
then shifted in dismay
at witnessing
its friend turn back
to shelter from the gray.

It knew that this
storm, too, shall pass,
and yet felt frail and jilted.
Then sun came through,
the ground dried,

but its flowers remained wilted.

The breeze felt colder
than before,
and autumn fell its leaves
onto its fading borders,
careless of
a Path that grieves.

Then, mudding
into green's decay
while longing for its friend,
it vowed to freeze
with winter's chill
'til meeting once again.

Luna (Ode to the Divine Feminine)

Oh, timely Goddess, is this truly a curse?
Is this Blessing?
Ancestral karma?
Worse?

Like a tragic comedy,
through the laughter,
they promised I'd be pained,
disregarded,
left alone and stained...

Brought up to believe that
We should be ashamed,
We lost our sense of Divinity,
as preordained.

Hell hath no fury like Woman scorned
and taken for the Love she'd once contained
for everyone who called Her Name.

See, I sat with Eve.

And I ate the Fruit.

And I conjured Lilith,
and Her Truth...

So misunderstood,
but disillusionment is glorious gift
 - one Heaven sent.

A heartbreak I've both felt and seen.

I'm blessed to listen to Her dream:
Though fallen,
still hopeful to Redeem
and to come clean.

I've beared Life,
and I've lost it, too.

I've chosen most that I've been through.

Though tides have ebbed and took my Youth...
Stolen my voice and left me mute...
I deconstruct,
    then I reboot.

Such disconnect that took my feet
and dropped me, naked, in the street,
left me abandoned with conceit

by those who came just for receipt...

Found Adam's grievance carried on,
as rib once Given, now is gone,
becoming weak what once was strong,
confusing Love with siren song.

His Divine nurture stripped from him,
and offered passage into "sin",
and he took it...

But he would again,
for Women are creators of Men.

Some will seek, some go astray,
some vie to strip night from the day
and break us down
   and tie us down
      and shut us up
         and run away.

We must not fray.

Bearers of Fruit,
Gardens of Loving respite,
We gently guide day into night
and fill the moon
with Divine Light.

Let us call on Gaia for insight
to help Us set things Right:

"Oh, Gaia,
I'm ever more aware
how much my Heart and Roots need care,
but do I have the Strength to spare?
What must I change to see repair?

What can I grow if I Surrender?
What must I learn?
What will I remember?

And though this Fruit is mine to share,
Please, Gaia, tell me when and where.
I will be on time.
I will be there."

She answers Us.
  She always does.
    No silent treatment...

UNCONDITIONAL LOVE.

Birthed from service,
 with attention to every detail,
with comprehension of every exhale
  and why it's given...
so that We may not suffocate,

but rest
and labor
and Recreate.

I see the tides now returning Flow,
as I walk paths only Mothers know to pave
just for my feet to go
and help my inner Goddess grow.

And, Luna...
Sweet, Loving, Infinite Luna...
Dancing on waves
and diving through the deepest of waters,
We remain your keepers,
and your most grateful Daughters.

Give Us Strength.

Please,
give us Ease.

Light our Paths in the darkness.

Lift us from our knees
so that, even in the wildest
or stormiest of seas,
We may be equipped
to facilitate
Peace.

Of Codependency

A stepping stone
on my way Home
looked up and smiled at me...
Engraved across,
a cursive message,
"Love and Let It Be".

I cursed it back
then went on walking,
searching for defense
of anyone
or anything
fear sought to work against.

I'd seek to teach
those within reach,
though they were not receptive;
Through their aversion
that I learned
that fear can be deceptive.

I pushed those that
I Love away
by overstepping bounds,
for trying to change another

is futile
off common grounds.

Yes, I was
on a mission
to be Keeper without keeping
awareness of
the void within
and unhealed wounds left creeping.

I thought that if
I gave enough,
then chaos would be stilled;
but empty cups
can't pour at all
without being refilled.

Since Nature finds
a way of breaking
that which is not bending,
I'd find myself
shut down somehow,
and bound to my own mending.

It took so long
to realize
that I had been the reason
for every sickness,
every spell

that benched me for a season.

I've learned that Love
fades to control
with fear and expectation,
and can be felt
when giving starts
to render irritation.

That irritation,
once compounded,
then becomes resentment.
And resenting
anything
creates starved discontentment.

And once this feeling
builds a nest
inside my human frame,
it leaves disease
and restlessness
with only me to blame.

That stepping stone,
I understand,
was cautionary sign -
A gentle call
to fill my lamp
before I try to Shine.

For when I do,
I'm carried
to what's truly needing me,
and then my Love
moves mountains
with its authenticity.

And it is then,
as I give care,
that my Light only grows.
Where it once dimmed
while chasing fears,
it now reaps as it sows.

In learning how
to Love myself
and hold space without lack,
I've given space
to those I Love
to get themselves on track.

So, now,
if I feel hurt by them
not listening to me,
I look down,
eyes closed,
and remember,
"Love, and Let It Be."

Enneadic Fate

I Become
what I Believe

I Believe
what I Receive

I Receive
what I Accept

I Accept
what I Allow

I Allow
what I Create

I Create
what I Speak

I Speak
what I Feel

I Feel
what I Think

I Think

what I Choose

I Choose
what I Become

Manipura

there's Energy that
moves through the pits of my lungs
and trembles my core

tells me to listen
and pay attention to words
to actions, to eyes

tells me to slow down
examine between the lines
seek out intentions

tells me to recall
lessons of where I've come from
to know where to step

moves me to wonder
whether I'm on the right path
or stuck in the ditch

asks me to quiet
my brain and my anxious nerves
to sense what and how

it tells me to feel,

to be here Now and always
so that I hear it

reminds me to BREATHE
to fill with Purpose and Love
and exhale the rest

it tells me what's True
and all that I should avoid
to align with You

it tells me what Is
and all that will ever be
if I listen close

it knows what I need
it's always there to guide me
it is my Instinct

it is my power
my compass and clarity
it follows the Sun

it's my saving grace
it redeems my mind from fear
armor for my Heart

there's this Energy
where the diaphragm nestles

yes, you have it, too

I Heard You

I heard You
when You played the perfect song
in the most perfect moment
just for me to receive it,
just for me to have faith in Your plan for me,
and to remind me why.

You carried me through the rain
across town
to a place I'd never been:
a place that felt familiar, nonetheless.
a place scented warmly with comfort
and acceptance.
a place that felt like Home.

I heard You call me by my name
and out of my seat
to speak my Truth
to an audience of those waiting to listen.

I asked for this
and You gave so gracefully,
so coincidentally,
so brilliantly,
and in a way I'd not expected.

I heard You in my voice,
as I spoke the words
that I'd exhaled, cyclically -
once upon a dream,
once upon a lesson,
once upon a triumph of renewal
and surrender.

You echoed through the room
through the stillness surrounding me,
through the breaths and affirmations
in the sounds of the lovely souls
there with me...

through everyone
there
exhaling with me.

I heard You speak
before and after me
through all the others
there to share their stories
their minds
their gifts and understandings
their trials and errors
their losses and their triumphs, too.

You were there,

and all I could pray
was that this ambiance of Creation...
this Beauty,
this Wonder,
this glorious Light
from every eye and heart in the room
would burst through the walls
and echo down the streets
and cleanse the whole town
as a ripple that grows into a wave
washing over the Earth.

And once it all ended -
the wisdom
the regards and the musings
the offerings
and the gratitude
We'd gathered for that night,
You left with me,
as I know You left with them.

And I heard You
because You heard me first.

Thank You.

Inconvenience

According to many,
I am inconvenienced.

According to many,
from what I hear,
so are they:

"My appointment went on
                    too long.
There was a train.
I got cut off in traffic.
Someone else got in my way.
THIS STUFF ALWAYS HAPPENS TO ME.

The kids were up too late.
That one coworker just
                would

                    not

                    shut

                        up today...
Endless lines at the store!
And I found a hair in my
     homemade
        salad,
SO I THREW IT OUT.

I don't have food for dinner...
   my cabinets are full,
   my fridge is full,
   my produce basket, a graveyard
       for apples and seasonal stone fruit,
but I have nothing,
so I'll just STARVE.

My stupid hair won't stay in place,
My stupid pants don't fit today,
My back aches, and my car won't start,
   and my whole day fell apart
       when I had to call so-and-so,
         and they put me on hold
             for FORTY-TWO MINUTES...
                 SAVAGES...

   Life SUCKS, and I'm over it."

Well, I've been inconvenienced
   - like, FORTY-TWO TIMES -
in the time it took to write these words,
 BUT...

Sometimes,
We're moved out of harm's way.
Sometimes,
 We're saved from what we can't see

like a traffic accident
  or a derailing altercation
  or even just from ourselves.
Sometimes,
We're needed elsewhere unexpectedly,
 and we end up at the most right place
  at the most right time.
Sometimes, we're challenged
  to create a new routine,
    to find a new job,
      to think a different way,
        or to simply slow down
          and count our blessings...

And sometimes...
 ALL the time...
   if we spend our lives complaining,
    thinking everything so draining,
     the Universe is listening...
       our Reality is listening,
        hanging on every word and every tone,
       like a child first learning a language.
      It hears our words as wishes,
    like a clever genie, freed of his lamp,
and back to teach us a clever lesson.

For what we focus on the most
  is what is then created
    and increased,

47

as though it's EXACTLY
    what we'd asked for...
And in so many ways, it IS.

What we give attention is what grows.
And, how we react
determines whether or not it blooms.

Is your garden full of Love?
Is the soil well-nourished?
Are you Grateful you have one at all?
Are you Thankful for the flora?
Are you Hopeful for the fruits?
Are you teaming up with Nature?

    Or is tending and watering it
            just
         another
      inconvenience?

Of Narcissism

I see you in the lime light so often,
soaking up the adoration,
reveling in the greatness
of your performances.
And I see you backstage
before each and every show,
preparing to depict your very own take
on tragic romances.

Oh, I see you,
there at your lipsticked mirror,
blotting and caking your face,
meticulously covering every discrepancy
that may be seen at a distance
under a halo of halogen glow,
creating this leading role
of deific inerrancy.

Yes, I hear you reciting your words
over the voices of cast and crew,
and berating them
for not doing exactly as you say...
Using some just to assist you,
coercing some to do better,
and screaming at others

to get the hell out of your way.

And I feel the breakdown
and reconstruction of the language,
as it filters through
the imperious fears of your brain,
sharpening to barb wire
as it rolls off your tongue
to seek out the next host
to bind and drain.

And I know, as well as you do,
that fifteen seconds runs out
far more quickly than you'll
ever choose to accept.
And I know, as well as you do,
that once the curtain call is over
and the house clears out,
you'll stand alone, in the dark, inept.

And I know that you'll keep
kissing that reflective glass,
averse to making any eye contact,
counting on the very next show
to fill you up, redeem your power
and permit you to own the stage
and everyone on it, yet again,
as the audience applauds your glow...

But, no...

No, I did not come here for your autograph.

I've only come to ask:

When the ticket sales cease,
when that mirror finally shatters,
and when all your fed-up castmates
have marched off your stage,
what
are
you
left
with?

Well, I know,
as well as you do,
that That's all that matters.

Heartbreak

What do You do with heartbreak
when it tears You from your self?
What do You do with heartbreak
when it strips You of your health?

What do You do when your heart
trembles through your shaking voice?
What do You do when your Love
wanes by their own quaking choice?

What do You do when Love You give
is subject to rejection
by one so perfectly imperfect
asking for perfection?

What do You do when one You Love
starts dimming their own Light
to pull themselves away from Love
and keep it out of sight?

What do You do when You know
You were brought here for a reason,
if your beloved changes face
with any trying season?

What do You do when signs
alert You to their every need,
but darkness casts its chill over
each propagated seed?

What do You do when there is
nothing left that You can do,
but pray for them, and for yourself,
to carry You both through?

You let go; Love them, with respect
for space that is required.
You pray for them, and Heal yourself
as You've always desired.

Our Time is short, and Time is lost
with resistance sustained,
and You will understand one day
You were, with Purpose, pained.

For Love we seek from other souls
is oft what we yearn for,
but You will learn through gift and loss
that there is so much more.

Yes, there is so much more to You
than what You give to one.
Your Love is LIMITLESS,
and there is more work to be done.

Oh, heartbreak comes to change us,
but here's what I pray for You:
that You will find Love for yourself
and Peace and Patience, too.

Forgiveness

I remember.
I surrender.
I release,
and I forgive.

Though it hurt me,
though it changed me,
I still need me.
I still live.

I have Purpose.
I have Power.
I create the
way I feel.

Though it shook me
from my Center,
I let go so
I can Heal.

What I cling to -
what I carry,
poisons or
regenerates.

When I use
history as weapon,
Presence then
disintegrates.

I release myself
from burden,
so I can be
my best me.

Present moment
is deserving
of complete
tranquility.

The pain of Then
needn't be Now.
It needn't be here
to relive.

Though I remember,
I surrender.
I release,
and I forgive.

Two Different Paths
(Enter the Wolves)

The winter held
on stubbornly
that dark and dreary year.
The ice clung
to the landscape
as a coward clings to fear.

The wooded Path
looked downhill
to its silent, frozen friend,
then slunk back
into shadows,
unaware of how to mend.

Illuminating
only now and then
had proven errant;
connection lost and
strangling vines
grew ever more apparent.

Then, suddenly,

a rustling in the distance
caught its eye...
one white as light,
one black as night -
two wolves were passing by.

Their scars
and muscles, highlighted,
o'er calloused, timeless feet,
displaying wounds
from battles lost
and strength birthed through defeat.

Their breath -
harmonious exchange
of wind and warmth and song,
brought an awareness
to the Path
of where it first went wrong.

The fears that bound
its trail from Flow
created such resistance,
no other Path
could be permitted
peaceful coexistence.

The wolves then found
their way upon

the Path's remaining space,
but, here, they began
to dispute
which wolf decided pace.

A narrow, cluttered
path does not
give near the space that's needed
for two souls
seeking to align
without one superceded.

The Path watched this
and realized
adapting is requirement
for Nature
to facilitate
and bring all to alignment.

And as the sun
peeked through the trees
and brought the Path some light,
the Path decided
widening
would save the wolves the fight.

So, once it widened,
both the wolves
then joined each other's side,

and, as though
they'd never stirred,
absolved themselves of pride.

They stepped over
the rocks and vines,
all while the Path remembered
its friend who'd once
implied great gifts
come from complete surrender.

It watched the wolves
walk toward the Light
and cross beyond the treeside
and came to see
that fear had led
the first time that it tried.

It missed that
once sacred connection
it had come to know
before its friend
had beckoned it
to join the River's flow.

The wolves then rested,
head to foot,
and warmed the frozen ground.
The Path

down by the water
thawed a bit and felt less bound.

The winter's ice
broke down the vines
and fortified the pass,
and spring broke through,
as wolves' breath thawed
the foliage and grass.

The lighted Path
looked up the hill
and saw, to its surprise,
its sheltered friend
spreading Its way
with confident reprise...

Now understanding
rains would come
not to deter Its gains,
but to replenish
and restore
and wash away Its banes.

And so It bravely
moved down toward
Its newly restored friend
and joined It by
the riverside

to co-create and mend.

Both Paths in Light
then spoke with Love
of every season squandered.
They spoke of storms
and ice and wolves
and Balance, as They wandered.

These two Paths, now,
have become One...
I hear They're spreading still.
For what's been lost
is always found
through Patience, Love, and Will.

I Know You

In the way You challenge me -
In the way You show me -
In the way You teach me -
I know You.

In the way You carry me -
In the way You vie for me -
In the way You reach me -
I know You.

I know You
as I know my Home,
      my Vessel,
      my Children
      my Garden...
   in the way my spirit beckons,
     and is Grateful, for each pardon...
   in the way I feel assurance
     when You're dutifully regarded.

I know it's You
that flushes the soffit of my skin -
   an inversive embrace of
   restorative tides rolling in -
     with that Gratitude...

with that Grace...
with a cleansing intervention
that washes me
from crown to base
and reminds me
You're still with me.

You're
Still
Here.

So, I carry You
as You carry me,
And I breathe You
as You breathe life into me,
And I speak of You
as You speak through me,
And I dance with You
as You keep rhythm for me,
And I preserve You
as You watch out for me,
And I know You Now
as You've always known me,
And I Love You
as You Love...

Unconditionally.

Sol (Love Letter to the Divine Masculine)

Shining confidently through
  the windows of my soul -
    Your rays, with fervent accuracy,
      piercing through my core:
    bearing Logic
      bearing Strength
        bearing Patience
    and an emboldened Security
      of Balance that effortlessly insights
      an endless warmth and clarity
      that repairs and transmutes
        the weakness birthed
          from a long night's shadow...

These beautiful and mystical
  and reliable Good Mornings of You -
    The gravity of You redeeming
      the depravity in me,
    washing over me,
      moving through me,

steering all of me...
over
and into
and beyond me.

The Warrior in You
  brings out the Warrior in me.

Reaching down,
     beams of unmatched resilience
          pulling Life from decay then
     healing all from crown to root,
my Protector.

You shine down so fiercely
  from the heavens,
     filling us with Faith
          in the gifts of Tomorrow.

Centering Yourself
     to be the very center
          of all that Is.
The Guardian
     of the Nurturer
          of all that Is.
The Co-Creater
     of the Foundation
          of all that Is.

Your Logic
    - to serve enlightened resolution.
Your Strength
    - to lift the weak to restitution.
Your Patience
    - to comfort grief to absolution.

You cast spotlight over dear Luna,
   as She carries us from dusk to dawn.
      You warm the belly of Mother Gaia,
         as She cradles us in song.
            You lift and nourish Your children
            in ways that neither can,
And You are needed
  for Your Wisdom
    and safe authority
      and infinite resolve
  to return fortitude and conviction
    to the Hearts of every woman and man.

Please, be with us.
Now, and ever more.

Potential

I invite you to sit back,
and think of everything We could be -
if this world, if our Spirit
was exactly as it should be -
full of Life, free to Love,
boasting Happiness and Health?
We would want just what We need.
We'd consider this our wealth -
not the money, not the power
over others, not the fame,
not the status, nor the ego
used to put others to shame,
but compassion! And to do this,
we must reach down deep within.
We must open up our minds,
as we absolve every sin.
Like rebuilding after storms
that have torn our worlds apart,
We must cast aside our differences
and work to Heal the Heart.
Education holds the answers -
not mere textbooks on a shelf,
but the kind you only find
when you go searching for Yourself.
We must look to our tomorrow -

to what lies ahead, and trust
that corrections are still possible...
that We all simply must
pull ourselves back to our feet
and brush off centuries of debris.

But, 'til then, I will stand strong,
and speak of all that We could be.

To My Children

For every time I've been blessed to see
the Light in your eyes
when you've looked up to me,
I just want to say Thank You
for shining my way
and for birthing this Love
that I carry each day.

For every second I've watched you arise
from the discouragement
of your so many tries,
I just want to Praise you
for not giving in
as you try to keep learning
and aiming to win.

For every moment I've lost time with you
due to busier times
or obstruction of view,
I just want to say sorry
for not being there
and that time spent without you
can never compare.

For every instance that you surprised me

by showing me Grace
when you could have despised me,
I pray that you see -
in a world full of hatred -
that you are a Gift,
for forgiveness is sacred.

To my Son:

You are vibrant
and valiant and Free.
You inspire me to play
far more effortlessly.
Your laugh is contagious
and so is your glow.
You bring so much Joy
everywhere that you go.
Your resilience and Courage
deserve commendation.
You give Love and Kindness
without reservation.
Please, always remember
that you are so smart.
Never stop asking questions.
Stay true to your Heart.
Please, keep yourself Humble
and Loyal and sweet,
and never forget
that you came here Complete.

You are here to move mountains,
and shake some up, too.
I'm excited for everyone
who'll get to know you.

To my Daughter:

You're Beautiful!
Always remember,
even when your fire
reduces to ember,
your Light is forever,
your Spirit is magic,
and your Strength will see you
through anything tragic.
I'm blessed just to watch you
grow through every trial,
to then come out with Wisdom,
still donning that smile.
Please, keep telling your jokes,
and keep searching for Truth,
and never let growing old
steal from your youth.
You were brought here to challenge
and change and Create.
You were given a Power
no one can deflate.
Please, never give up,
even through Life's extremes,

and let nothing impede you
from chasing your Dreams.

No words can express
all the Love that I feel
for you, my dear children...
There's nothing more Real.

I vow to stand by you,
support you and guide you
and be there to Love you
for all that's inside you.

For all that you Are
and for all that you'll Be,
you have my whole Heart
unconditionally.